I0408057

Unless...
The Case for a Return to Common Sense

By Richard L. McBain

Printed in the United States of America
Triune Group, Inc. – Publishing
Library of Congress Number Pending
Copyright © April 1, 2017
By Richard L. McBain
All Rights Reserved

ISBN-10:1546555056

Richard L. McBain

Table of Contents

PROLOGUE

By Richard L. McBain
Copyright © April 1, 2017

*"*Common sense - is a basic ability to perceive,
understand, and judge things that are shared by
("common to") nearly all people and
can reasonably be expected of nearly all people
without need for debate; a type of basic awareness
and ability to judge that most people are expected
to share naturally"* *Wikipedia – the free
encyclopedia

There was a time in the United States when civility
was ever-present, knowing and caring for your
neighbors was a big part of life, and common sense
made "political correctness" completely
unnecessary.

Current day narcissism, and putting oneself before
others existed way in the background of society,
and thereby held very little need for "safe-spaces",
and the "snow-flake" generation that appeared on
the scene around 2010 or so. "Snow-flake" is a

derogatory term used to describe young adults who

want to take offense at views different than their own.

These misguided young people will soon find out that safe-zones don't happen outside of their pathetic liberal based colleges and universities. The real world will be extremely difficult to these feather-weights, and they will have only these incompetent so-called schools of higher education, and selfish parents to blame for it.

"Snow-flakes" are the product of basically two very troubling situations. The first is the lack of parental training, accountability, and inexcusable lack of love, through inattention and little time devoted to child rearing in the home. The second is the poor quality of education and lack of discipline found in an overwhelming percentage of our public school systems, and the horrible tenets of a run-amok progressive-liberal college institutions.

Heartfelt belief in God is at an all-time low in America, and is now even mocked as ridiculous by many who think that they know better. These foolish people see themselves as so intelligent that

they dismiss the truth of God out of hand, because

their little pea-brains can't understand what is not obvious to them.

Modern technology has all but wiped out the need to learn interpersonal skills, and kids today don't know how to react, negotiate, read body language, or even empathize or sympathize with friends and others they come in contact with.

This book is intended to identify the abhorrent directions that society in the United States, and in fact the world, has taken over the last five or so decades. The anecdotal stories and comments are written to help the reader clearly see that the fun and closeness of a society of years ago is gone for good, **Unless...**

Richard L. McBain

CHAPTER ONE
Changing Skewed Values

"Come on Tommy, let's go outside and play some catch", Tommy's Dad said. It's really nice outside, and we should be enjoying some outside time. "No thanks Dad, I'm texting with a couple of friends right now", Tommy explained. "Okay, maybe later" his Dad responded.

Mr. McCall walked into the living room where his wife was reading a book. "You know Nancy, I'm worried about Tommy and all his texting, Facebook, and tweets. He never seems to want to do anything outside, but just stay in his room with his tech stuff and continually having conversations with his friends without any personal contact", he said to his wife.

"I know, I'm worried too; kids today have no idea what fun they're missing by getting out and playing with their friends, Mrs. McCall said. "I

wonder what has changed so much from our childhood days that so many kids today have no idea what fun we used to have outside with our friends playing baseball, or hide-and-seek, riding our bikes, flying kites, and ice skating or sledding in the winter", commented Mr. McCall. All of those fun times we had for all of

those years have just disappeared with kids today; I wish there was something we could do to bring back those time for our kids" said Mr. McCall. He lowered his head in regret, but then a thought hit him; "Unless…

The thought Mr. McCall had was that maybe he could bring back those fun times for his kids and others by spending the necessary time planning and leading them in outdoor activities. As he thought about it he realized this could really take some time, but also thought that time spent on his kids to try and change their ideas of fun was important enough to invest himself in it. He decided to do it.

It was Spring and baseball season had begun, so Mr. McCall spoke to his two boys about putting together some softball games so some of the girls would play. Tommy his twelve year old didn't seem over excited about the idea, but his younger boy, Jimmy who was ten liked the idea.

There was a park at the end of their road about three blocks from their house, and it had three baseball fields for the local little league teams. Mr. McCall told his boys that they would need at least twelve kids to put two teams together. He asked the boys to come up with a list of both boys and girls that they thought might be interested in playing.

He called the park manager and asked if they could use one of the fields when not in use for the little leaguers. The manager told him that field three was almost always available because the number of teams playing in little league had diminished over the last few years. Mr. McCall thanked him and told the manager they would be out on Saturday morning.

Mr. McCall found out that changing the direction the kids had been going in was more difficult than he thought. The lack of interest in just playing softball didn't seem to pique many of the kid's interest. He decided to skip the first Saturday, and make his son Jimmy's birthday a party at the park. He had the boys tell all of the invitees to bring a glove for softball. Mrs. McCall called all of the invited kid's parents to inform them of the time, and that there would be a cook-out and a softball game.

The day came and as the different friends began showing up, Mr. McCall would motion that he was going to throw a ball to them. They quickly put on their glove and began catching the balls he was throwing. He lavished praise on the kids who were catching the balls, and also for those throwing them back. He quickly had those who showed up first take the field, and began hitting balls to them. Before he knew it, the kids were getting into the fun, and throwing to each other.

After about forty-five minutes or so he called them in and said, "Okay kids, let's pick teams and play a game, what do you say?" They were all for it, and he showed them how to throw the bat up vertically, and the team captain would grab it, and she and the other team captain would go hand over hand to the end of the bat to see who would pick first.
There were fourteen kids that showed up, so two

teams of seven were picked, and then tossed a coin to see who would take the field first. Fortunately a number of the parents decided to stay and see the game, and Mr. McCall asked some to help with umpiring.

The game lasted an hour, and everyone was really having a good time. They then grilled out hot dogs and hamburgers after the game, and had cake and ice cream to celebrate Jimmy's birthday.

When the party was over, the kids were relating what a good time they had, and wished it wasn't over. Mr. McCall then announced that he would be happy to give a couple of hours every Saturday here at the park, if the kids would come and play softball. A couple of other dad's said they would help, and the kids all agreed to come.

Changing the direction of our children takes some time and effort on the part of caring parents to get their children out of the house to play. Children

love attention from their parents, and by leading their kids into fun activities outside, they can bring back what many of us elder folks saw as normal.

The physical presence and contact with other children will greatly aid them in life in dealing with tough situations, negotiating, and learning how to read body language. If children remain solely connected to others through technical and social media, they will miss all of those people skills needed in dealing with the world outside of school.

Parents need to be parents and not friends of their children. It is their responsibility to limit and monitor cell phones and social media, television, and the internet. There is a wealth of harmful garbage on all of the media, and children can easily get porn sites, dangerous chat rooms, and become the victims of pedophiles, and other violent criminal just on their telephones alone. Parents must search and find competent ways of blocking and monitoring all of this media, and reminding resistant kids that they are the parent and that they are the provider of them.

There are huge numbers of children posting nude pictures of themselves and others on Facebook, Twitter, and the internet. Many of the younger kids don't realize the danger involved, and may have been dared by friends or bad people they are in contact with. Once posted, their pictures are out there for life!

Child suicide and attempted suicides have increased immensely. Depression in our children many times is from lack of parental attention and direction. Of course, some suicides and attempts are related to mental illness, but most are due to basic needs not being met, and no belief system in God or His love for them. It is also important to know that many doctors have been carelessly throwing drugs at our kids for misdiagnosed ADHD, and child maladies, without proper diagnosis. Common senses clearly says that parents need to stop their doctors to take the time to explain why the prescription, side-effects, and long-term problem possibilities; it's the parents duty!

Allowing young children to "hang out" at Malls, arcades, and other places predators frequent is very dangerous. It probably was the same when I was a kid, but ever so much more nowadays. If kids are allowed to go places of concern, they should be made to be a part of a group, and that group must be told not to let singles wander away.

Many kids are not doing well in school, and one of the big reasons is parents not doing their part with homework. All parents should have a clear line of communication with teachers to be able to periodically check on their child's progress at school, and to be sure that they are doing their homework. Quality time with the kids can often be helping them with their homework, but not doing it for them. They will never learn if someone keeps giving them the answers!

If you haven't been giving your children much attention, you need to know that no matter what they say, they crave the love of their parents. Being resistant to an immediate change may be what some kids do, but keep at it knowing your love is needed. You are not a good parent until you take some quality time with your kids; those who do this will quickly see the rewards, but make no mistake, kids will definitely go the wrong way

unless...

Unless...

CHAPTER TWO
Spiritual Necessities

No one can deny the two forces we see every day in society and the world. Good and evil are easy to differentiate, and should be clearly understood as much more than just human beings doing nice or bad things to each other. Both of these are rooted spiritually in people, and thereby create the need to deal with the evil aspect.

The problem that people have in really understanding these two forces is derived in their level of spirituality, or lack thereof. It is easy to understand that non-believers in God simply don't buy into spirituality because they think that all we have is the here and now, and that physical death is final. They think that they are superior in their minds over God- believers, and ignore the wonderful creation that they believe came from some ridiculous and discredited "big bang" theory, and evolution from that point; they are truly foolish people!

"The fool has said in his heart, there is no God"

Psalms 53:1

A more disconcerting problem are the hundreds of millions of people who claim to know God while not having so much as a clue of who He really is, what He expects from us in obedience to Him, and how to appropriately fight evil. Twenty-three percent of the entire world population believe in a false God, and the teachings of a false prophet who made it up as he went.

Most of the Jewish people are still waiting for the promised Messiah who actually came in His first visit to earth some two thousand years ago. The majority of them then and now denied that Jesus was the promised Messiah, because they were confused by scripture and expected the eternal kingdom of the Messiah to be set up when He comes; they missed or confused the scriptures about a second coming to do that.

As with many, if not most of religious groups, the Jews seem to band together more as a great historical people, than attached to the Mosaic Law they purport to believe. They have received great hatred over the centuries for several reasons. The first has been jealousy brought on by being God's chosen people.

The second is the blessings of God making this people possessors of shrewd business acumen, and a knack to thrive and stick together. Unfortunately the Jewish people have mostly become disillusioned over time, just as they did many times in the past when God pulled back from a "stiff-necked and gainsaying people." However, God promised to save the remnant, and will return for those people.

We also have had many cults, usually led by deranged people recruiting weak-minded folks to follow them, while gaining power, wealth, and self-aggrandizement. A good example of real evil present in a cult was the Charles Manson "family" in the 1960's.

Charlie Manson was completely deluded in teaching his followers that a Beatles band song named "Helter Skelter" was a description of a race war, apocalyptic in nature, and that his cults murder of nine innocent people would begin that war. Manson embodies the very meaning of "Demon Possessed".

Now we come to the huge number of so called Christian people, who have managed to divide themselves up in massive numbers of confused "denominations". These divisions came about mostly due to corrupt leaders who became power hungry, and wanted their own following to bring them power, wealth, and control.

Catholicism for one has gone in and out of periods spreading the gospel of Christ, and then coming under the influence of corrupt Popes authorizing the murder and elimination of heretics, as they called them. These corrupt leaders began with the idea that a Popes decision about the church policies was directly given by God, thereby all but solidifying heresy if one disagreed.

Next came the "deification" of Mary the Mother of Jesus, and all of the fallacies that go along with it, including praying to Mary and other deceased saints to intercede for people. Jesus clearly told the Apostles to pray to the Father in His (Jesus) name. The Lord's Prayer was an outline for prayer, instructing in proper principles of praying.

Mary most likely holds a prominent place in Heaven, but was human. Praying the rosary or to deceased saints who reside in Heaven does no good. When we can pray directly to the Father in Jesus name, why would anyone want to side step that? The reason is that over the centuries many Popes, Cardinals, Bishops, and Priests have given doctrines of men that
are not of God.

Howbeit in vain do they worship me, teaching for doctrines the commandments of men.
Mark 7:7

A seminal figure of the Protestant Movement, Martin Luther, was a Catholic theologian, priest and monk who strongly disputed the doctrines of indulgences. Indulgences at that time were supposed gifts or benefits the Catholic Church's leaders could sell to decrease a sinner's time in purgatory, before going to heaven.

He also taught that salvation and eternal life was a free gift of God' grace to those who had faith and believed in Jesus Christ as the redeemer from sin, and not earned by good works. He was labeled a heretic by Pope Leo X, and excommunicated.

The Catholic Church has had a number of evil Popes and leaders as well as good ones, who adhered to the Gospel, and moved the church forward. Unfortunately though the Catholic Church uses their Bible in which the New Testament is the same as the Protestant Bible, most of their leaders have never promoted the reading and study of the Bible, which could lead to many questions of Catholic doctrine.

The Christian denominational list seems endless, when there is one truth, one God, and one plan of salvation. Some of these are very good at leading people to the Lord. Some are more social gatherings where you can believe anything that you want. Some extol the Baptism of the Holy Spirit and operating in Spiritual gifts. Very few purport the need in dealing with evil, and deliverance from demonic forces, mostly because it's scary to those who don't know their authority.

Thus we return to our original premise of this

chapter which was dealing with evil in order to free the captives, heal the sick, and commune with the Holy Spirit of God. The fact is that most people are afraid of the deeper truths taught by Jesus, and His expected ministry that He established for believers to do. They shun things that they don't understand, instead of looking into it through Biblical study time, and discussions with other believers.

Pastors in most churches today have watered down the gospel in order to not cause controversy, and lose their members. The loss of their members would mean less tithes and offerings, and how would they be able to continue without them; now where is the
faith in that?

When the Gospel is watered down, and church members don't hear the deeper things therein, the chances of dealing with evil or even understanding how to deal with it becomes a non-starter. Many Christian denominations do not believe in, teach, or even acknowledge the very _scriptural_ gift of the Baptism of the Holy Spirit. This is a special anointing of the power of God to live the Christian life, and the Apostles were told by Jesus not to go out into the ministry until they had received this anointing.

Many Pastors teach that this Baptism in the Spirit was for the Apostles only, which is ridiculous. The anointing of the Holy Spirit is necessary for believers to stop attacks of Satan and his demonic forces Jesus went on to tell the Apostles to teach all to do the same things as they do.

And I will pray the Father, and he shall give you another Comforter, that he may abide with you forever; John 14:16

But the Comforter, which is the Holy Ghost, whom the Father will send in my name, he shall teach you all things, and bring all things to your remembrance, whatsoever I have said unto you. John 14:26

[14] Afterward he appeared unto the eleven as they sat at meat, and upbraided them with their unbelief and hardness of heart, because they believed not them which had seen him after he was risen. [15] And he said unto them, Go ye into

all the world, and preach the gospel to every creature. [16] He that believeth and is baptized shall be saved; but he that believeth not shall be damned. [17] And these signs shall follow <u>them that believe; In my name shall they cast out devils; they shall speak with new tongues; [18] They shall take up serpents; and if they drink any deadly thing, it shall not hurt them; they shall lay hands on the sick, and they shall recover.</u> [19] So then after the Lord had spoken unto them, he was received up into heaven, and sat on the right hand of God. [20] And they went forth, and preached everywhere, the Lord working with them, and confirming the word with signs following. Amen. Mark 16: 14-20

There are a number of denominations that either wish that the sixteenth chapter of Mark was not in the Bible, or even teach that it was added later thereby voiding its accuracy as the Word of God. These same denominations then take the very clear and plain scriptures about the Spiritual Gifts listed in Corinthians and say that those were only for the Apostles. It is this kind of nonsense that has made innumerable Christians weak and not prepared to deal with evil as they should.

I was raised a Catholic, and from as long as I can remember had the understanding that Jesus was the Son of God, and God the Son who died for our sins and rose from the dead. I understood this not only from my mother teaching me this, but just felt such a love for God that I never doubted.

The problem came when I was in high school, and began drinking beer, smoking, cussing and fighting, but still loving the Lord. My friends even called me preacher because I was talking about the Lord quite often.

The Catholic church and their schools that I was brought up in never taught us that the Lord wanted a personal relationship with us, or that we should study the Bible as the Word of God. In fact I was taught that the Bible was a good book that contained some of God's Word, but that much of it was just writings of men.

During my combat days in the jungles of Vietnam, I prayed regularly, and even called for a priest to come out and serve Mass whenever it was safe to do so. We would stack up wooden ammo boxes for the altar right in the middle of the jungle.

When I returned home I was married and had two boys. I had been smoking marijuana for eight years, and drinking a lot, but I knew something was missing. I began to realize that I had moved away from my beliefs, and fell away from the Catholic Church. I still believed wholeheartedly in the Lord, but as in high school was once again "living like hell".

I finally bought a Protestant King James version of the Bible because I knew I was doing wrong, and wanted to learn more about God. When I read it, I just wasn't understanding or getting a lot of it. My younger brother Bob began asking me to come to this Bible study with him on Tuesday nights. After giving him many excuses and not going, I finally went with him. That night I sat in a room of mostly Southern Baptists and some Catholics, and watched with amazement as these men spoke about the Bible, and its being the literal Word of God.

At the end of the study that night, they asked me what I thought about all that I heard. I said I would like to believe like they do, but in reading the Bible, I wasn't seeing what they saw. They quickly told me that I need the Baptism of the Holy Spirit.

When I asked what that was, they walked me scripturally through it. Really wanting more of God I said I wanted that. They prayed with me with the laying on of hands, and a language I had never heard began to flow out of my mouth. I had never heard tongues before and I was amazed as it was me speaking it.

My life took a one hundred and eighty degree turn that night, and I became truly on fire for God and literally hungered for His Word. Then miracles began happening and I was floored that God would do these things for me. I shortly thereafter realized that He will do them for any who step out in faith and believe His Word.

This is the scriptural truth for fighting Satan and his demonic forces. This special anointing of God called the Baptism of the Holy Spirit is not just a onetime event as some say, but an ongoing anointing to live the Christian life. The proper interpretation is "...be being filled", and I ask the Lord to fill me or Baptize me with His Holy Spirit every day.

And they were all filled with the Holy Ghost, and

began to speak with other tongues, as the Spirit gave them utterance. **Acts 2:4**

The above scripture clearly shows this anointing was not just for the Apostles as there was some three thousand there that day. Another one of many accounts of others being baptized or filled with the Holy Spirit was in Joppa, where a Centurion was told by an angel to send for Peter, which was then unlawful for Jews to go into a Roman's house. Peter told them all about it salvation through Jesus Christ, and the anointing of God.

[38] **How God anointed Jesus of Nazareth with the Holy Ghost and with power: who went about doing good, and healing all that were oppressed of the devil; for God was with him.** [39] **And we are witnesses of all things which he did both in the land of the Jews, and in Jerusalem; whom they slew and hanged on a tree:** [40] **Him God raised up the third day, and shewed him openly;** [41] **Not to all the people, but unto witnesses chosen before God, even to us, who did eat and drink with him after he rose from the dead.** [42] **And he commanded us to preach unto the people, and to testify that it is he which was**

ordained of God to be the Judge of quick and dead. [43] To him give all the prophets witness, that through his name whosoever believeth in him shall receive remission of sins. [44] While Peter yet spake these words, the Holy Ghost fell on all them which heard the word. [45] And they of the circumcision which believed were astonished, as many as came with Peter, because that on the Gentiles also was poured out the gift of the Holy Ghost. [46] For they heard them speak with tongues, and magnify God. Then answered Peter, [47] Can any man forbid water, that these should not be baptized, which have received the Holy Ghost as well as we? [48] And he commanded them to be baptized in the name of the Lord. Then prayed they him to tarry certain days. Acts 10: 38-48

It is this very anointing which is called the Baptism in the Holy Spirit that gives the power to deal with evil. Sickness and disease are evil and are actually demons, but if you tell non-believers that, they think that you have lost your mind. Well if we call ourselves Christians, that means we believe the teachings of our Lord Jesus the Christ, and He is our main example to follow.

Now when Jesus healed so many, what is recorded much of the time about Him doing this? He first called out the demon(s) that were causing these afflictions, then told the people being prayed for to be healed!

When the even was come, they brought unto him many that were possessed with devils: and he cast out the spirits with his word, and healed all that were sick: Matthew 8:16

And he healed many that were sick of divers diseases and cast out many devils; and suffered not the devils to speak, because they knew him. Mark 1:34

And they cast out many devils, and anointed with oil many that were sick, and healed them. Mark 6:13

And they that were vexed with unclean spirits: and they were healed. Luke 6:18

And certain women, which had been healed of evil spirits and infirmities, Mary called Magdalene, out of whom went seven devils,

Luke 8:2

They also which saw it told them by what means he that was possessed of the devils was healed. Luke 8:36

When Jesus saw that the people came running together, he rebuked the foul spirit, saying unto him, Thou dumb and deaf spirit, I charge thee, come out of him, and enter no more into him. Mark 9:25

Then was brought unto him one possessed with a devil, blind, and dumb: and he healed him, insomuch that the blind and dumb both spake and saw. Matthew 12:22

And his fame went throughout all Syria: and they brought unto him all sick people that were taken with divers diseases and torments, and those which were possessed with devils, and those which were lunatick and those that had the palsy; and he healed them. Matthew 4:24

Scripture tells us that every believer has authority over the enemy, but without being sure and filled with faith, and the power of the Holy Spirit, people can find themselves in a situation where they are in way over their heads. Remember the sons of Sceva?

[13] **Then certain of the vagabond Jews, exorcists, took upon them to call over them which had evil spirits the name of the LORD Jesus, saying, We adjure you by Jesus whom Paul preacheth. [14] And there were seven sons of one Sceva, a Jew, and chief of the priests, which did so. [15] And the evil spirit answered and said, Jesus I know, and Paul I know; but who are ye? [16] And the man in whom the evil spirit was leaped on them, and overcame them, and prevailed against them, so that they fled out of that house naked and wounded. Acts 19: 13-16**

This is the very reason that the Christian churches must not falter in teaching and training their members about the Baptism of the Holy Spirit and spiritual gifts which are to be used when dealing with evil. Otherwise the Pastors will be responsible for throwing their flocks to the wolves without being equipped to fight properly. The Word tells us clearly:

[10] Finally, my brethren, be strong in the Lord, and in the power of his might. [11] Put on the whole armour of God that ye may be able to stand against the wiles of the devil. [12] For we wrestle not against flesh and blood, but against principalities, against powers, against the rulers of the darkness of this world, against spiritual wickedness in high places. [13] Wherefore take unto you the whole armour of God that ye may be able to withstand in the evil day, and having done all, to stand. [14] Stand therefore, having your loins girt about with truth, and having on the breastplate of righteousness; [15] And your feet shod with the preparation of the gospel of peace; [16] Above all, taking the shield of faith, wherewith ye shall be able to quench all the fiery darts of the wicked. [17] And take the helmet of salvation, and the sword of the Spirit, which is the word of God: [18] Praying always with all prayer and supplication in the Spirit, and watching thereunto with all perseverance and supplication for all saints;   Ephesians 6: 10-18

So now it comes down to just plain common sense for us individually and as a church to be sure that we are equipped to fight evil, which will get continually worse until the second return of Jesus. We have the authority and the anointing if we ask for it, and can strengthen our faith by studying the Word of God; everything we need for dealing with evil.

Now we must reassess our part in what Jesus calls all of us believers to do. By knowing the way to be equipped to fight evil, and stop its primarily unopposed spread in our family and friends, our real enemy Satan will begin to lose time and time again. He lost the war already, but battles still rage on unbelievers and those who don't know or won't learn their authority to combat him. We all can stop much of what he is doing, **Unless...**

Unless...

CHAPTER THREE
The Need For Patriotism

Every strong country over the ages has eventually come to upheaval and societal changes that have destroyed the foundations of their originations. Many of these countries very much needed revolution to remove despots and evil from their leadership.

The United States, as young as it is, has been able to weather these problems through a strong and fair constitution the country's founders established. There were years of debate about becoming independent from England, but once decided by the majority the revolution began.

Winning the Revolutionary War and becoming its own sovereign nation, the framers of the constitution found the way, and created a document inspired by scripture that became the new laws of the land.

There have been several groups who have tried to divide and destroy this country and radically change the Constitution, but have failed. The Civil War of the 1860's came close, but the union of the country stayed in place.

Today we have a much more dangerous and very subtle movement of evil trying to take over the country that is the example to the world of benevolence and good, and destroy its foundations from within.

The United States is the envy of the world, and yet so many have become unpatriotic and are working to change our society from capitalism and competition, to socialism giving everyone a free ride and living off of the government. These Godless people refuse to see that everywhere socialism has taken root, it has ruined country after country and has never worked.

This evil movement constantly looks to change the Constitution through appointment of judges who make decisions by political ideology and try to "legislate from the bench". There are now appointed justices of the Supreme Court that do this, and in their decisions thwart constitutional principles.

We have foolish senators who proclaim that they believe that the Constitution is a living and evolving document, which would make it open to changing the very system of government and our lives to the whims of corrupt elected officials. Many of the protests we see are not good and lawful, but are perpetrated by paid, violent bullies who disrupt, destroy, and attack any group or people disagreeing with them. They organize through incitement on social media and bring people out who think they have a right to protest violently and hurt anyone getting in their way.

I believe that the United States needs to bring back the military draft where every able bodied youth is forced to serve two years in service to their country. Military discipline will greatly aid in reshaping the liberal brainwashing they have been getting in school, and teach them that there is a more important aspect to life than just themselves. God help us if another world war breaks out and we are not prepared with Patriots in our ranks.

The draft ended with the Vietnam War. I was

drafted out of college because I fooled around and flunked out my Freshman year. I was afraid of the war and so got back in quickly and was on the deans list when I was drafted. Unfortunately for me it was too late; once you lost your college deferment, it was gone.

I did not believe in the Vietnam War at all, and my brother John was there before me. However I did believe in my country, and knew if everyone who didn't believe in something they were called to do by their country didn't go, we would have nothing but anarchy. I have always been a patriot and we must put the good of the whole above individual fear or selfishness.

Patriots need to stand up and fight for what they believe in. The lawful way to fight has many aspects, and doesn't mean fist fighting these paid thugs at protests. The first way to fight is to not be lazy in educating ourselves about what is going on, and voting against the corrupt politicians who are ruining our country.

It is clear common sense to look and see that since our country began, elected officials over time abuse power, and forget what they are there for. Allowing our representative to be embedded in the government for twenty, thirty, and forty years is foolish, and allows them to become lords instead of servants. So many of our politicians are in their eighties, and stumble with words and thought; time to remove them.

People need to stand up and join groups who will be a force for term limits. The congressmen and senators need to be held to term limits, just as the President. The entrenchment of politicians who mostly enrich themselves through lobbyists and make their decisions on the money backing them need to be thrown out of our leadership.

Standing up for what is right against the evil that is trying to destroy our country in necessary for anyone calling themselves a Patriot. This last election I believe was ordained by God, and we will see much of the terrible decisions made by the former administration turned back around. We can all be a part of this **Unless...**

Unless...

CHAPTER FOUR
Our Deteriorating Education System

The United States education system hasn't ranked number one in our high school and colleges in over twenty years. Back then the returning G.I.'s from World War II had become seasoned thinkers, and the G.I. Bill gave them the opportunity to develop desired careers, which they eagerly went after.

Our public school system is loaded with incompetent teachers who have become so liberalized that they are <u>suspending grade schoolers</u> for ridiculous reasons. Recently young children have been suspended for using their hand and forefinger in making a figurative gun symbol; Idiotic! One student was suspended, yeah suspended for drawing a gun on paper. Is their any brains in these so called teachers?

A huge problem is the NEA teachers union that protects incompetent teachers from being fired, gives huge amounts of money to the DNC and liberal organizations, while almost nothing to conservative causes in education.

When I was in grade school we had show and tell times to display our favorite Christmas gifts. I brought a two gun holster set from the cowboy days and no one thought a thing about it. Today I would have been suspended or sent to juvy. and my parents would have been arrested for letting me bring these dangerous implements to school.

There seems to be no level of common sense in most of our school systems, and teachers that object are ridiculed, suspended, and even fired for stating a differing view. The Liberal-Progressive Movement is purposely defunct of common sense, and instead injects evil ideology into one of their main tenets which is not to allow dissenting debates.

Our poor education system needs to rethink just plain common sense ideas to better the system. Provision of much more teacher training would be a good start, as long as it is coupled with common sense procedures, and reasonable discipline to maintain order. Next the school system Principal's and Administrators must back up their teachers with the real discipline problems, and hold their parents accountable for their children's unruly behavior.

Reduction in class size can be very helpful, and school systems need to make room for more classes when what they have becomes too big for one teacher to handle. All schools, but in particular inner-city schools should look at budgeting enough money for a significant security team, preferably armed to deal with the "Gang-Bangers" who come and sell drugs and disrupt classes while terrorizing teachers.

All school systems in the United States need to be forced to teach American History, Civics which is the duty of citizenship, and American Government. Youth today have little to no knowledge of these subjects, and the reason is obvious; they are not being taught such! English needs to be the only language that is spoken in schools, other than teaching foreign language classes for those who want to learn them.

A great number of our Universities are training the students that the government owes them an education, health care, food and other freebies, and has taken competition totally out of the equation. They have established safe-zones for the poor little college students who may be offended...by anything! In the past few years they have been labeled "Snow-Flakes" for this petty, immature way of doing things. They will all find out they have been lied to by the school system when they get out in the real world expecting everything, and getting nothing.

Parents in the United States are much to blame. They have not prepared their kids in common sense beliefs, and are extremely careless in selecting, or letting their kids select their own colleges. When most parent's witness what is happening on the campuses where their kids go, they just stay out of it preferring to let these corrupt schools indoctrinate their children in ideology that will not work in the real world. Shame on them!

These same parents are either not aware, or don't care that the extremely liberal so called professors are not teaching them American History, or about capitalism, or about the competition they will face outside of their little safe-zones.

Academic Tenure is a ridiculous concept, defunct of any common sense in a society that is competitive or merit based. It allows teachers and professors to lifetime appointments without fear of firing except for just cause. A vast majority of these so called educators have been teaching precepts of progressivism and socialist doctrines, and most are intolerant of any discourse in their classes.

Our schools, and especially our university systems are supposed to encourage expanse of thought and debate of ideas, and not shutting them down to one way of thinking. The safe zones these institutions have created to quell debate are hurting our kids intellectually and emotionally by functioning only until they leave school. There is just no common sense to this!

With the destructive protests happening all over America's campuses, law enforcement must step up with debilitating tear gas, pepper spray, and water cannons, and let these punks know that there is not going to be any toleration for violent protests. Innocent protestors will just need to flee out of the way, and let police arrest these violent paid thugs.

Our education system is filled with immoral, unlawful, lying evil people, and together parents and government can rid the system of them, **unless...**

Richard L. McBain

CHAPTER FIVE
Does Anyone Know What Morality Is?

"Morality is the differentiation of intentions, decisions, and actions between those that are distinguished as proper and those that are improper.[1] Morality can be a body of standards or principles derived from a code of conduct from a particular philosophy, religion, or culture, or it can derive from a standard that a person believes should be universal.[2] Morality may also be specifically synonymous with "goodness" or "rightness".

*Wikipedia – the free dictionary

If nothing else, a nation's culture determines what is moral or not. The United States was founded on Judeo-Christian principles, and morality was defined early on by a nation whose majority was churched and believed in the Bible.

Over the years this country had censorship boards beginning in the early twentieth century. These boards proliferated as the movie industry continued to test the waters for producing movies that were considered immoral. Huge movements by women's organizations fought against the influence on impressionable youth of movies that were hurting their morals, health, and belief systems.

For decades Hollywood has been a bastion of immoral, evil- doing people by calling their junk art; what a joke. There were great movies made early on, and even a few today, but most are laced with graphic violence and sex, foul language, nudity, and wholly unbelievable filth that they call art. I'm sure most actors and actresses have no spiritual belief other than false religions that they find or even establish to say it's okay to do all of their immoral behavior.

A proper question to ask would be is there anyone outside of Hollywood and Atheist beliefs that graphic sex, murderous violence, vile filthy language, and disrespect for those in authority is immoral? Unfortunately, the answer has become yes over the last thirty years or so. Most Americans watch some of these shows, and the use of vile language has become almost common, not to mention immoral disrespect for Authorities.

But chiefly them that walk after the flesh in the lust of uncleanness, and despise government. Presumptuous are they, self-willed, they are not afraid to speak evil of dignities. 2 Peter 2:10

My third book, A Reluctant Warriors Combat Memories is about my combat experiences in the jungles of Vietnam in 1969-70. I was asked to write it in a screenplay, which I did. A President of a studio in Hollywood called me after reading it and said he loved it. He told me it would cost about fifty-million dollars to make the movie, and a writer could get a million dollars for it.

As we talked he was a big help to me, and gave me suggestions about improving the story including hiring a writer to help me get it great. After forty-five minutes, he finally told me that we would have to "commercialize" the story. I asked what that meant, and he said that he had noticed there was no bad language in the screenplay, or my book. I told him that I had used some of the worse language that can be spoken while in the war, but my Christianity now caused me to leave it out.

He went on to tell me that investors need to make twice as much as they invest in the movie, and that they wanted realism because that's what sells. I told him I would not put bad language in the movie, and asked him about John Wayne movies not having any. "Dick" he said, "that was another time and place". Anyway, I was pleased that he had called me, but there was no amount of money I would take to displease my Lord.

I say that most of this garbage called art is extremely evil, and obvious to see if one believes the bible. To wit:

Let no corrupt communication proceed out of your mouth, but that which is good to the use of edifying, that it may minister grace unto the hearers. Ephesians 4:29

[22] Professing themselves to be wise, they became fools, [23] And changed the glory of the uncorruptible God into an image made like to corruptible man, and to birds, and fourfooted beasts, and creeping things. [24] Wherefore God also gave them up to uncleanness through the lusts of their own hearts, to dishonour their

own bodies between themselves: [25] Who changed the truth of God into a lie, and worshipped and served the creature more than the Creator, who is blessed forever. Amen. [26] For this cause God gave them up unto vile affections: for even their women did change the natural use into that which is against nature: [27] And likewise also the men, leaving the natural use of the woman, burned in their lust one toward another; men with men working that which is unseemly, and receiving in themselves that recompence of their error which was meet. [28] And even as they did not like to retain God in their knowledge, God gave them over to a reprobate mind, to do those things which are not convenient; [29] Being filled with all unrighteousness, fornication, wickedness, covetousness, maliciousness; full of envy, murder, debate, deceit, malignity; whisperers, [30] Backbiters, haters of God, despiteful, proud, boasters, inventors of evil things, disobedient to parents, [31] Without understanding, covenantbreakers, without natural affection, implacable, unmerciful: [32] Who knowing the judgment of God, that they which commit such things are worthy of death, not only do the

same, but have pleasure in them that do them.
Romans 1:22-32

The news media has been getting away for years
with false reporting of stories they make up or
exaggerate about, seemingly "quoting" people or
events that they have absolutely no evidence of.
Most of these so-called journalists have given up
reporting factual news, and anything that goes
against their liberal agenda, to not reporting big
stories that would bring into question their huge
bias; this is immoral!

Thank God we have a President who is the first
one to call them out, and point out their bias on a
regular basis. The news media are in a dither and
very upset that someone who has the ear of the
American people is finally making it clear about
the garbage they are reporting. They are beside
themselves as are the Liberal-Progressives that
they lost an election they thought they had in the
bag, greatly due to their fake news.

Sol Alinsky, the founder of the community
organizing which Obama followed as an organizer,
taught progressives that they should do anything to

get and hold power; whatever is necessary. Hillary Clinton wrote her college thesis on Alinsky, and then we were told by Jeffrey Ziefman that he fired her on her first job for being an * "unethical and dishonest" lawyer. Unfortunately she did not learn a lesson because she has been lying ever since.
*Fox Nation February 25, 2014

Immorality in our families is at an all-time high. Some studies show that eighty percent of American marriages have an unfaithful partner, and now many of these are the wife. The evil feminist movement has worked hard to subvert the God ordained family order with the man earning the living, and the woman raising their children.

The narcissism and self-serving behavior of America's children can be linked easily to the feminists proclaiming freedom from man's domination by mothers going to build a career rather than raise their children. The kids as a result are missing the nurturing love of a present parent, and in fending for themselves with just money thrown at them, have learned to be selfish and uncaring about others. This is immoral!

Many studies have repeatedly shown that the family is the foundation of a society, and when parents are seeing to the training of their children in good Godly spiritual values, a country remains strong. When a country's family foundation breaks up, societies become weak, misled, and usually will fall apart. Whether you are a believer or not, Satan and his evil forces are hard at work to destroy our foundations, and have been successful in destroying many strong countries before us.

The majority of parents have stopped taking their children to church, or involving them in anything spiritual. Without this training, the immorality just continues to grow, and the adhesive that holds families together weakens and eventually falls apart.

One in every three children in the United States is now born to an unwed mother. A growing number of people believe that the chance of a successful marriage is so low, why even bother getting married. Society has made divorce so easy that the marriage vows are simply recited for the ceremony with no understanding what a vow is; a solemn promise under God.

Pastors especially need to counsel betrothed men and women in the commands of God, and how sacred marriage is to Him. The moral slide of the United States has been slow and methodical. When I see the changes that have come to pass after the last sixty years, it is not only obvious, but downright disgusting and based on the presence of evil we have allowed to materialize.

The internet is a mixed bag of good and evil. On line people can find the Bible, Christian teachings, health and medical information, reviews on books and programs, and a plethora of other interesting and valuable information. Unfortunately we can also find pornography, vile satanic rituals and information, fake news, false and evil narratives about adultery being good for a marriage, personal character assassinations, terrorist training, and the list goes on.

The good news is that God gives us a free will to choose our paths, including what we say, read, watch, bear witness to, and in this country the ability to speak up for those beliefs. Contrary to common sense conversation and debate of ideas is Political Correctness.

*The term **political correctness** (adjectivally: **politically correct**; commonly abbreviated to **PC** or **P.C.**) in modern usage, is used to describe some language, policies, or measures that are intended to avoid offense or disadvantage to members of particular groups in society.
* Wikipedia – the free encyclopedia

In mainstream political discourse and media, the term is generally used as a pejorative, implying that these policies are excessive. Author Dinesh D'Souza's 1991 book *Illiberal Education*, in which he condemned what he saw as liberal efforts to advance self-victimization, multiculturalism through language, affirmative action, and changes to the content of school and university curricula.

Political Correctness is generally used as an excuse to quell common sense discussion and debate, and used to protect groups of people from something that may be offensive to them. The whole idea is absurd, and if people are "thin-skinned" that they are offended from common discourse, then go run to your little safe-zones where you won't have to hear it. They will remain ignorant of what is really going on in the world, only protected by such ridiculous liberal thinking. Oh I'm sorry, that was not PC!

What is immoral about Political Correctness is that it breeds unrest and hatred purposely used to divide us as a nation of equal people, and creating a festering evil of social unrest, while pitting one group against another. It is truly a term straight from hell!

All of the degeneration of morality in this country has been allowed to happen through apathy, misleading by our leaders and the news media, and a growing lack of spiritual training and Bible study. We can turn it around with some effort and mind set changes, and by speaking out common sense values, **unless...**

Richard L. McBain

CHAPTER SIX
Our Laws Are To Be Obeyed

First of all the United States is a Republic, which is a government where sovereign power is vested in the people. The United States is a representative government where the people elect officials to represent what they want in a larger governing body. It must be said that since our beginning as a country, most of the elected officials have forgotten this premise and have let the power they were invested with by the people to go to their head, and have allowed that power to become corrupt, usually for their own power, self-aggrandizement, and path to self-wealth.

Political parties were formed to group together elected officials with similar ideologies so that they would be stronger than the other groups, and get their ways. Today both parties have forgotten their way, and evil has become clearly evident in the Democratic party. They lie continually then turn around and accuse the Republicans of being the ones doing it. They fabricate stories on fake news and innuendo to smear those who ardently

disagree with them.

A case in point is the ridiculous allegations of the
Trump administration colluding with the Russians
to win the election against Hillary Clinton. The
Dem's take illegal surveillance the Obama
administration most likely ordered, where some of
Trump's campaign staff had regular meetings with
the Russian Ambassador just as Obama and Hillary
had, and make it look like collusion possibilities;
they knew it wasn't true but had their friends in the
media make the American people think it was.

Even worse was the Benghazi debacle. Obama and
Hillary Clinton propagated a lie for weeks about
the attack on the embassy, and killing the America
Ambassador to Libya and special forces protectors,
by blaming it on a video that they knew the next
day was not the cause. Then lied to cover up the
incompetence of Obama and Clinton for not
sending help; evil!

As usual, there was no accountability for these
blatant lies and in my mind, criminal refusal to
send help. Let's not forget that the Ambassador
had requested more security for weeks before the

attack, and Clinton turned him down; now he is dead!

The blatant disobedience of the laws of our country can once again be found mostly in the Democratic Party and their ridiculous explanations for breaking the law. Our laws regarding immigration, violent anarchists, police protection, negotiating with terrorists, holding countries that provide terrorist safe-havens accountable, tax laws, and so many more are clear to see, but what has been done about it?

As with all things regarding our government, common sense should be our guide. Our Immigration laws allow a million immigrants to become legal permanent residents per year. There are also tens of thousands of immigrant's to come here and work on time restricted visas. This is common sense, and meets the needs of our countries growth and labor initiatives. It also serves as a protection against terrorists coming in to try and hurt Americans.

Legal immigration requires vetting, which is thorough investigating and scrutinizing people wanting to come into our country before letting them do so. We have found over the decades that our open boarders do not facilitate legal immigration, but allow mass illegal immigration, bringing with it criminals, drug dealers, and terrorists bent on destroying the American way.

Again, the Democratic Party wants this law flaunted, and wants open immigration. Let's be clear that they don't do this out of the kindness of their hearts like they falsely claim, but to add to their voter base to win elections. Clear thinking people can see this is true by what has been happening with the illegal Hispanic immigrants.

First the Democratic Party wants no voter ID laws so illegals can vote. Second they want them given Drivers Licenses so they can look legal when they do vote. The way they gain these illegal immigrants allegiance is by what they do for them.

Democrats are great at the semantics game. Instead of the title illegal immigrant, they insist that they are just undocumented people. They insist that these illegal immigrants' children be schooled and taught by Spanish speaking teachers. The cost to our school systems is horrendous and should not be allowed.

Democrats further want all illegal immigrants to be eligible and receive citizen benefits like food stamps, welfare, health care and the like all at the taxpayers' expense. There is certainly no common sense here.

Sanctuary Cities and now a state blatantly break federal law by not holding criminal illegal aliens for our federal authorities. These leaders of these cities and state should be charged and put in jail for breaking the law, but again, there is not any accountability for doing this.

As a result I submit that these bleeding heart liberals should welcome these illegal aliens into their homes, and we'll see how long they last. But no, Liberals want all of this illegal stuff done, as long as it doesn't affect them.

Politicians who for years believe that they are above the law, readily break lobbying laws, lie under oath, smear others who don't agree with them, which is slander, and leak classified information to the media when it will help their cause; no accountability.

Oversight committees in the Congress and Senate have become emasculated by government agencies who refuse to comply with their requested, or to provide even subpoenaed documents and information under investigation; no accountability.

Politicians enrich themselves by using campaign contributions for themselves and their family. Some family members working the campaigns have been paid $300,000.00. How much gets kicked back to the candidate? Just how many politicians are elected to an office with not much money, and come out wealthy has been hard to determine because of the evil lying, cheating, and stealing going on by them. We the people are accountable to quit putting these law-breakers back in office with each election; if we don't, we get what we deserve.

Mayors and Governors tie the hands of their police who risk their lives to keep us safe. It's the Democrats who alone support groups like Black Lives Matter, an anarchist movement with police in their sights. Common sense tells us that police must be able to quell violence with whatever means is necessary to do the job. Tear gas, water cannons, stun-guns, and rubber bullets should be used to control these violent protestors, and imprisonment for such behavior.

The Advice and Consent portion of our constitution concerning federal judges allows the Senate to investigate and make a finding if the candidate is qualified to fill that role, not if they go along with the ideology of one party or another. Attempting to do otherwise is a violation of constitutional law.

Perjury has happened many times in our government, and again sees little to no accountability. President Bill Clinton lied many times about his extra-marital affairs, and was brought up on charges that he lied under oath.

He was impeached but acquitted because the needed votes of 60 to remove him from office were not there. Not one Democrat voted against him, instead, they all went to the Rose Garden of the White House, and gave Clinton a standing ovation for thwarting the law. An attempt by Republicans to bring Clinton to justice failed due to the corruption of liberals; evil!

Crime is rampant everywhere, and especially in our big cities. District Attorneys ignore the penalties described by law and let bad criminals confess to a lesser charge. They do this because it's easier, and they don't have the help they need in these DA offices to handle the load. Bad people are let go with a smack on the wrist many times, and they are out here doing it again, and again, and again. New prisons need to be built, and DA offices need bigger budgets to hire more attorneys to handle these blatant breakers of the law.

Without accountability to our laws, all we have is constant chaos. There is a way to change all of this if we will only do our part. Everyone must have the name, phone number, and e-mail address of their political representatives. These are very easy to get on-line, and then keep them and send e-mails or call telling them what you want them to do.

Once again, all of this mess in this country is

mostly due to plain and clear evil. God wants us to do our part, and we can see a huge difference, **unless...**

Richard L. McBain

CHAPTER SEVEN
Evil Of The Feminist Movement

**"For the time will come when they will not
endure sound doctrine; but after their own lusts
shall they heap to themselves teachers, having
<u>itching ears</u>; and they shall turn away their ears
from the truth, and shall be turned unto
fables."**   **(2 Timothy 4: 3-4)**

The primary evil in the Feminist Movement is their
promotion of abortion to end unwanted
pregnancies. The great problem we have is that
heavenly law trumps earthly law. To anyone who
can't see the common sense of killing babies while
unborn, I say their whole premise is selfish and
directly against the Word of God! For those who
are unbelievers in Jesus Christ and God's Word, I
pity you.

Many have espoused that it is legal in the United
States, but it is never legal in God's court. Whether
you believe or not doesn't change the reality of
eternal life or death. Many naysayers are
unfortunately burning in Hell for killing God's

children.

**"Listen, O isles, unto me; and hearken, ye
people, from far; The Lord hath called me from
the womb; from the bowels of my mother hath
He made mention of my name."** (Isaiah 49: 1)

**"Did not He that made me in the womb make
him? and did not one fashion us in the womb?**
                                    (Job 31: 15)
**"Lo, children are a heritage of the Lord: and
the fruit of the womb is his reward."**
                                    (Psalms 127: 3)

The next evil in the Feminist Movement is the
ridicule and belittlement of homemaking mothers.
The Creator set the world order, and if a married
couple decides to have children, that decision
should include the mother staying home and
raising the children. The obvious reason for this is
to be there offering the love and affection and
training young children need.

My wife, who had worked until our first son was
born, made the selfless decision to stay at home
with him rather than pursue her career. She went to

school at night when I was home with the kids, and occasionally took a part-time job a couple of nights a week, and Saturdays, just to get out of the house once in a while.

Our sons have always been grateful for their mom being there for them, and even their friends who would come to our house after school where Jackie was and appreciated her; some even called her mom. Unfortunately, my wife was looked down on when she would get into women's groups, because she "didn't work". What Jackie did was ever so much harder than any of their careers, and our kids had what they needed.

Many women I spoke to, mostly employees, when by themselves would tell me they envied my wife for being able to stay home with the kids, and wished they could; but in a group of women they mocked women who stayed home. Ridiculous!

Daycare will never offer anywhere near that need for individual children, and parents have been lying to themselves about this for some time. Feminists make women feel that work is their right and the way to go, while God says just the opposite. And women who abandon their children to daycare know good and well it is usually for selfish reasons, and for increasing income to live a higher-life at the expense of their children.

Single mothers may have to work, especially widows who don't have much choice. Unfortunately most single mothers caused their problems with pre-marital sex, or divorce without taking all of the necessary steps to prevent it.

"The wise woman builds her house, but with her own hands the foolish one tears hers down (Proverbs 14:1)

The Feminist Movement becomes incensed for anyone who espouses that the man should be the head of the household. The most important thing to remember is that we are to serve one another, and not lording our positions over one another.

God put men in charge of the household because He chose to. Many feminists have a fit over the Bibles' descriptions of God's social order, but forget that someone has to be in charge, and that everyone can't be totally equal or we would get very little accomplished at all.

"But I would have you know that the head of every man is Christ; and the head of the woman is the man; and the head of Christ is God."
                                        (1 Corinthians 11:3)

"For the man is not of the woman; but the woman of the man. Neither was the man created for the woman; but the woman for the man."
                                    (1 Corinthians 11: 8-9)

Discussing God's priorities with other women can have a reversing effect from the feminist movement. Most women today, after decades of propaganda from this movement, really have begun to see that much of the movement is a fallacy. They have been losing numbers of people in this movement over the last few years due to the untruths coming to light.

We should be ever aware of the sins of pride and selfishness, that if given expression, will cause us to fall from God's will. We will find real peace and joy by putting God first in our lives over all other things, especially those that sound good but are contrary to His Word.

We need to take notice of how unhappy and militant many members of the feminist movement are. They are mostly complaining, plotting, and demonstrating continuing their attempt to get attention for their movement. "...By their fruit we will recognize them..."

The fact that most of the feminist movement's issues go against God's will, and that they are misleading many, is not the only problem. It's the climate the movement creates, even with those who do not subscribe to it. Over a period of time, things that seem blatantly wrong become accepted, because they are packaged in ways that seem good, but are not.

Christians must not affiliate themselves with the feminist movement, and especially abortion. Once again it is imperative for the Christian to remember that America's laws are not always God's laws. People who call themselves Christian and promote, or affiliate with those who promote abortion, are guilty of murder no matter what the feminists say, and will answer to God for it.

The obvious evil in the Feminist Movement should be very clear to see, and allows us to be free from those sins, **unless...**

Richard L. McBain

CHAPTER EIGHT
Need For America's Legal System Accountability

Another huge need for common sense is in our legal system. There is certainly no common sense in taking non-violent, first-time offenders and sentencing them to harsh, long prison sentences without heinous circumstances involved.

Unfortunately the other end of that is incompetent judges letting off repeat, violent felons with a "hand slap", and putting them out on the street to do it again. When this blatant disregard for our laws and the need for real justice happen, I submit that the offending judge should be sentenced when the criminal they stupidly let off does it again; that would be accountability. With laws made for this kind of accountability, we would see this junk stop quickly. People say we can't do that, and I say that we certainly can!

Next we have the judges, justices of courts of appeal, and supreme court justices legislating from the bench. They have absolutely no right to do that, so where is the accountability? They totally ignore the laws on the books because of their ideology, and because who will stop them? Juries find violent murderers and the like guilty and they are given the death penalty. The bad joke is that they are given twenty or more years on death row, and allowed to appeal their penalty. The time for execution comes and some liberal judge legislating from the bench discards the jury verdict, and commutes the sentence to life imprisonment. This should not be legal!

No one should ever be executed for anything but concrete evidence, and never based on circumstantial evidence. Evidence that is circumstantial has been found wrong many times later on, so life imprisonment should be the punishment until or unless other concrete evidence is produced. DNA evidence today has both exonerated formerly convicted and unfortunately executed people, but has also closed the door on any other doubt in cases that had been uncertain.

It is the solemn duty of our congress to create laws that will hold these rogue so called judges and justices accountable for breaking the law by ignoring it in their decisions.

There is a way to make this happen, and it takes very little effort by all of us. Congressmen and Senators should be called regularly, e-mailed, tweeted, and posted on Facebook, and any other media possible to let them know what we want. It is just as important that you ask friends, family, and other contacts to do the same. Constituent pressure does have consequences, and town hall meetings should also be a part of informing them. Grass roots movements do change things!

Criminal law is only the beginning. Civil law is completely out of control, and we must continue to push for tort reform. "Tort reform refers to proposed changes in the civil justice system that aim to reduce the ability of victims to bring tort litigation or to reduce damages they can receive". (Wikipedia)

Litigation for everything and anything is so out of control it is not only ridiculous, but absurd! The main reason it goes on is that there is almost no accountability for frivolous law suits, and many innocent companies and individuals being sued will settle just because it's cheaper than to have these cases purposely get extended on and on. Judges need to use common sense and get to the bottom of these cases rather than let lying plaintiffs and attorneys hurt innocent people.

Two of my companies have been sued in the past, and our lawyers wanted to settle; I refused. They warned me that I could lose it all, and I said so be it; if truth and righteousness can't win, then I will go and do something else.

The first case was with a former stockholder and officer who had been embezzling from the company. I had him thrown out, and he sued us. What he didn't know, as I let him lie under oath, was that I had absolute proof of his guilt. When I produced it in court, the judge threw out the case.

The second case came from a new black female employee who I had told that all employees must be on time because of the service we provided. She told me no problem, and was late every day for her first eight days. Her branch manager tried to hide it from me, but I got wind of it and went over to that office and fired her.

She went to EEOC and filed a claim for racism. The EEOC made threats to me to settle, and I told them not a penny. An EEOC case worker came to my office, and I could see from her face and demeanor that she had already decided I was guilty without even meeting me. For her it was a simple racist thought in her incompetent brain that I was white so I must be wrong against this poor little lying black girl. I ended up reminding her that she was supposed to be impartial, and told her to get out of my office.

They subpoenaed me to come to the EEOC office, and began a settlement offer at tens of thousands of dollars. The man kept telling me that I could lose the case and it could cost me my whole company; what a fool! After six months and many threats it had come down to one thousand dollars; I told them not a penny. After a year, the EEOC threatened me one more time, and I said not a penny; that was the end of that.

Today in work environments people have become ridiculous regarding some comments made by the opposite sex. When paying a compliment becomes sexual harassment policies need to be reviewed. Men and women working together should be able to communicate without worry that something they say may be misconstrued. Levity in the workplace makes for a more enjoyable environment, but the PC police are always looking for wrongdoing.

Of course there are those who are crude and vulgar, and offend others without regard for their feelings or wanting to hear such things; this is never appropriate. However we have large numbers of people, mostly women who take offense much too easily, and need a clear policy written to spell out what is appropriate and what is not.

Here again we see huge lawsuits being filed by women who say they have been offended or sexually abused, but continue working under someone who they later say is the offender; sometimes years later, and want big settlements. Common sense would deny someone a settlement after a long period without saying anything, then bringing up something that happened years ago.

The point is we should never settle for something that we didn't do. It's almost funny that a third of the ads on television now are nothing but "ambulance chasers" seeking anyone who was hurt or wants easy money, whether there is really fault or not.

Obviously, those with fault should pay, but then the amounts get so ridiculous there is no justification. Plaintiffs get huge awards that amount to ten times or more than they could ever earn in a lifetime; how is that justice?

The need for common sense judgements is evident. There needs to be limits established that are fair, and juries in both criminal and civil cases need to be more clearly instructed. Findings by so many juries now days are ridiculous at best. They don't take their oaths seriously, and so many of their findings are plain stupid.

Juries who begin talking among themselves about the case before they are allowed to, are breaking the law. Some come to judgements before all of the evidence is in, which is also illegal.

People need to be held accountable in our legal system. Juries should have an independent supervisor who insures there is no prior collusion among members before deliberations are to begin.

Common sense should rule in our legal system regarding sentences, penalties, and monetary judgements. Of course all of what we have seen will continue, **unless...**

Unless...

CHAPTER NINE
Term Racism Ridiculously Misapplied

Racist - a person who shows or feels discrimination or prejudice against people of other races, or who believes that a particular race is superior to another.

Greatly due to Dr. Martin Luther King, Jr. and the Civil Rights Movement of the nineteen sixties, a giant step was taken to correct the injustices and abhorrent behavior and laws that had promoted racism for so long. These kinds of deep seated feelings certainly weren't going to change overnight, but gradually the premise of equality for all men and women in this country was on the rise, and was not about to be stopped.

Many African Americans felt things were moving too slowly at times, and who can blame them; there never should have been inequality based on color anyway. America was playing catchup with the given law of God, that all men and women are

created equal.

**Then Peter opened his mouth, and said, Of a truth I perceive that God
is no respecter of persons:
Acts 10:34**

[8] If ye fulfil the royal law according to the scripture, Thou shalt love thy neighbour as thyself, ye do well:[9] But if ye have respect to persons, ye commit sin, and are convinced of the law as transgressors.   James 2:8-9

A great deal of progress was made from the nineteen sixties through the early two thousands. Although there has been an element that thinks things will never be right, and blames their plight on the "White Man" instead of their own laziness and lack of educating themselves to get ahead in life, millions of African Americans have moved on. Huge numbers of college and high school educated Black Americans are professionals, and work jobs that have given them the American Dream! There is more opportunity for minorities now than ever before.

Unfortunately racism took a giant step backward

with the election of Barack Obama as President. The Democratic Party began an untrue mantra that anyone questioning President Obama was a racist. Then anyone questioning anything that the Democrats disagreed with were racists.

With President Trump's election, the Democrats have not ceased calling him a racist, while the likes of Maxine Waters and many others are the real racists. President Trump has made plans to do more for, and help the plight of the inner-city poor than the Democrats including Obama ever did for them; but he's racist they say.

Their evil is in their continually lying about everything and anything, then projecting their lying on their opponents. To continue to see and hear these poor losers misapply the term racist to anyone who disagrees with them is ridiculous.

Of course we have the charlatans who make their living and a whole lot more by race-baiting. One of the worst is the Reverend (choke, choke) Al Sharpton. He and Louis Farrakhan, Jessie Jackson, and many others continue to stir up the Black

Americans with continuous and absurd race baiting

while all along they are the real racists.

A vast majority of American people do not feel that Black Americans are anything less than themselves. There are certainly misunderstandings of different cultural traits that people of all races question about the others, but that is nothing more than questioning, or even making fun of at times, all because we see these traits differently and don't understand them. This is Human Nature, fear of the unknown, and when there is this fear we tend to make fun of or ridicule these things, rather than trying to understand them. These very same things happen between religions who don't understand the others point of view, as well as nationalities whose cultures are different.

Some black groups call for reparations for slavery. I would say reparations? Why reparations; were you there? Are you a slave? No of course not and the whole idea is ridiculous!

The hatred in America is at an all-time high, and those who seem to hate the most can't even tell you why. Common sense should tell us to take a

deep breath and reevaluate how we feel about our

fellow men and women. God said anyone who actually hates another is guilty of murder and will not go to heaven.

"Whosoever hateth his brother is a murderer: and ye know that no murderer hath eternal life abiding in him. 1 John 3:15

We can all stop this racism and hatred, **unless...**

Unless...

CHAPTER TEN

Richard L. McBain

Security In A Terrorist World

Terrorist - a person who uses unlawful violence and intimidation, especially against civilians, in the pursuit of political aims.

Terrorists have been around practically since the beginning of time, but today they are a plague worldwide, and have learned ways around our former security methods that provided safety. We have two classes of terrorist that we talk about; domestic and foreign.

Most remember the horrific domestic terrorist attack in Oklahoma City on April 19, 1995, that killed 168 people, and injured 680. It was a truck bomb that destroyed a third of the Alfred P. Murrah Federal Building, and was carried out by Timothy McVeigh and Terry Nichols.

From time to time we have faced other domestic terror attacks, usually by nut cases, and perpetrated on school students and innocent people in night clubs. The evil prevalent in these attackers is

obvious, and can only be stopped by others observing or hearing rants by these perpetrators, or reading their social media threats, or from personal knowledge.

Unfortunately, political correctness has once again interfered with people speaking up and warning the police about things they have heard. People now become more afraid of being made fun of and even ridiculed if they are wrong, than stepping out with information that may save lives.

A relatively new domestic terrorist group is the Black Lives Matter crew. Most of those cowards hide their faces in their violent protests, and do a great deal of physical and property damage where ever they appear.

Black Lives Matter was formed on a lie to begin with. Their untruthful "hands up don't shoot" movement against our police was a total fabrication, based on the shooting of the criminal Michael Brown. The lying so called eyewitnesses said he was shot with his hands up surrendering to a cop in August 2014 in Ferguson, Missouri. Although any killing is bad, this perpetrator fought

with the policeman, and tried to take his gun.

BLM (Black Lives Matter) continued this fake news about this shooting, and has skewed the statistics of police shootings of black people, where somewhere in the ninety percentile of black shooting that end in death are perpetrated by other blacks.

Once again, mayors like De Blasio in New York have tied the hands of police officers who risk their lives every day to protect us. Cops have become targets by BLM and the people they influence, and its time cops use more force against their violent protests. Gas, water cannon, and rubber bullets are a good start to disperse this anarchist movement when they become violent.

Common sense tells us all that there are always a few "bad apples" in any group holding power. I also tells us that you don't tie the hands of all for the few that abuse that power. President Obama and some Hollywood actors had quickly taken the side of BLM against our police. I wonder if they realize that they need the police to protect them also. What if the police didn't come when they are

attacked or broken into? No common sense there!

Other domestic terrorist groups are the cowardly fools paid to do violent protests. A good example is the recent attack on a college in Berkeley, California, to protest a conservative speaker. They started fires, broke windows, and hurt other people there, and all under cowardly masks of black. Some have accused George Soros of funding these violent protestors, but without proof there is little that the authorities can do.

Worldwide terrorism is currently out of control, and has been brought to our country numerous times so far. Beginning with the two attacks on the World Trade Center. Osama Bin Laden, the cowardly leader who sent large numbers of his followers on suicide missions, while he remained tucked away safely finally got what he deserved.

There are over one thousand Isis Muslim extremists under surveillance at this writing in the USA, and many more that are here that are not being watched. Sporadic attacks happen by small groups or lone people, all of which are hard to stop.

Along comes the bleeding heart liberals who are doing everything they can to thwart surveillance on

Muslims, and make security a nightmare for our authorities. Here again is where just plain common sense is needed to protect our country.

It amazes me how well our FBI and other security departments have done with one hand tied behind their backs. We all know that it is only a matter of time for the next horrific attack to happen here as they can't be everywhere and watching everybody.

The wall and border security needs to be continually presented as not so much to keep immigrants out, but to keep terrorists and drug dealers out. Probably thousands of terrorists have crossed our boarders illegally, and are living here awaiting orders or the right opportunity to kill Americans, and as many as possible.

I don't want anyone hurt, but when it comes, may it come to those who are the stupid, bleeding-heart liberals who are tying the hands of our anti-terrorist organizations. They are all for their ridiculous ideologies until it comes home to them, and then they are the first to scream for help from

the very organizations they try to emasculate.

Extreme vetting is the very least we should be doing before anyone enters this country. Since ninety-five percent or more of all terror attacks are done by Muslim extremists, profiling Muslims is simply common sense. If they don't have anything to hide what does it hurt? How many attacks and deaths will it take until people come to their senses?

We know of Mosques in this country that are training members and children in their schools to become radicalized and eventually kill the infidels. How stupid is that? All of these Mosques need to be closed immediately, and fall under these so called hate speech laws that liberals like to throw at anyone that disagrees with them. Wake up America!

Does the U.S. negotiate with terrorists? Yes it does, and it should not. Obama was not dealing in the interests of the United States when he made that horrendous deal with Iran. Everyone knows that Iran is probably the largest state sponsor of terrorism, and is absolutely responsible for

thousands of American lives. Why are we dealing with them? The Palestinians are controlled by

Hezbollah, a terrible terrorist organization, so why do we keep talking about a peace effort with them in the middle east.

One thing should be extremely clear; there will never be a lasting peace in the Middle-East. This has been going on for centuries, and to continue to talk about it, work at it, and make people think that this is even doable is ridiculous. Scripture tells us the story, and the hatred for Israel by the Palestinians, Iran, and many others will not end.

These Muslim extremists groups are purely evil, and the truth is not in them. It seems ridiculous to keep this charade of peace negotiations going with these total liars who have no thought of doing what they say. It is plain common sense not to continue with this so called diplomacy with evil players. It is laughable if anyone really believes that Iran is not working on an atomic weapon, and all of this facade that their atomic buildup is for electrical type power, when they have huge oil reserves is moronic.

The Taliban, which we have been fighting for over a decade is very much alive, and is just waiting for our pull-out from Afghanistan so they can re-take the leadership of that country. Isis is now wanting to join forces with them because so many of their fighters have been decimated by our air strikes.

However, Isis has many individual radicalized Muslims throughout the United States, and we have seen and experienced ourselves these so called "Lone Wolfs" who upon a whim, or in obedience to orders coded and given over the internet, attack and kill people.

Although it is frowned upon in many circles to speak of it, we can stop a great deal of this "Lone Wolf" terrorism if we arm ourselves. Many if not most states now have a licensing program for concealed weapons. When carrying a concealed weapon, it is imperative that we know how to use them. Shooting lessons are readily available, many through the local police departments like my wife and I took. After those initial lessons, it is necessary to go to the shooting range periodically to train.

I was a combat jungle veteran in Vietnam with the 101st Airborne Division, and I trained on just about every small arms weapon available at that time. However, over the years like anything else we become rusty, and need to retrain. I can't imagine anything worse than shooting an innocent bystander while trying to stop an armed terrorist. We need to be sure we can shoot straight, and that only comes with practice.

Of course many people want no part of this, and are uncomfortable around guns. Common sense tells us that people feeling that way should not be involved in arming themselves, but if only twenty-five percent of the citizens armed themselves and knew how to use their guns, we would see a lot of what has happened stopped before many, if anybody gets killed.

As was mentioned earlier, it is not fair to our police and anti-terrorist forces to leave it all to them. We all need to be ever vigilant, and when anything looks weird and out of place, there may be a good reason. Anything that looks troublesome should be reported. The police would much rather have you report something and be wrong, than to

not report it and people die.

We need to have a fast track appeal process to the Supreme Court of the United States, when these liberal judges who legislate from the bench, break the law. Several have recently held up legal Presidential regulations that are designed to protect our country from people trying to enter from countries that can't vet them properly. This is only common sense, and these judges, and courts of appeal need to be held accountable for their blatant breaking of the law!

The incompetence of some of these appeals courts can easily be seen in their previous decisions. For instance, the ridiculously liberal Ninth Circuit Court of Appeals in of course, San Francisco, have had eighty-six percent of their decisions overturned by the United States Supreme Court which shows we have some real dummies on the court.

It is my opinion that many people on both sides of the isle need to pass laws that can legally reduce the right to privacy for even citizens, who have given reason to our anti-terrorist agencies to

suspect terrorist activity. This of course should easily go for non-citizens and illegal immigrants who should have no citizen rights anyway; it's common sense!

We will never eradicate terrorism from the world or even from our own country, but we can put a huge end to most of it, **unless...**

Unless...

CHAPTER ELEVEN

So Called Journalism

It is important to understand what Journalism is supposed to be. There are many definitions nowadays, but several aspects seem to be in most of them. Simply put, it is supposed to be the "profession" of writing for newspapers, broad-cast news, magazines, and the like, in an unbiased way, to report facts and events of the day to inform society of such; that is what it is supposed to be.

Unfortunately so called journalists often forget what makes them professional, and choose to present many non-facts, innuendo, unprovable diatribes, and unsubstantiated rumors as truth. These are not journalists, but people with a biased agenda using their position to promote half-truths and outright lies.

Since the founding of our nation, we have had phony journalists like Philip Freneau, who operated and wrote for the partisan newspaper, The National Gazette. He worked with Madison and Thomas Jefferson to promote criticism of rivals,

purposely and untruthfully smearing the likes of George Washington and Alexander Hamilton.

The power that much of the media possesses as the vehicles that deliver the news, also brings with it the constant temptation to skew the information to meet the political agenda's of their owners.

Reporting the news in an impartial way to insure all sides are presented fairly, is why we call journalism a profession. Biased reporting is not professional, but instead is just another source of propaganda hiding within what is expected of the consumers.

"Fake News" has become the expression of the day when it comes to unsubstantiated, rumor-based diatribes from organization, many of which used to be legitimate news sources. So many of Americans still think they are getting accurate reporting when reading large newspapers like the New York Times, or viewing once respected television news from the main stream media.

The New York Times in my opinion, has become nothing but a liberal rag, and NBC, CBS, ABC,

CNN and MSNBC reports only what they want their viewers to hear; withholding information that would go against their political agendas. So now, journalism has become evil, lying based reporting from these liberal-progressive organizations, and they are too stupid to see that their loss of readers and viewers is due to this fact, or just don't care at all.

The Fox News Channel has understood what good journalism is, and they call it fair and balanced, letting people make up their own minds. They certainly can be seen as "right-leaning" because the majority of their reporters and anchors seem to be conservative, but the difference is that they present both sides. As a result their viewership has grown immensely, while their competitors continue to lose viewership; you'd think they would wake up!

With the popularity of the internet as a news source, newspapers may soon be a thing of the past. They can't compete in the instant news market, and people can explore and get the kind of news coverage they want, instead of the bias of the paper owners.

The Atlanta Journal, a paper I subscribed to and spent large sums of money years ago on my company advertising, went the way of the NYT, and became a liberal rag also. I canceled my subscription, as did many, and although new management came in saying they were going to report both sides, I haven't seen it.

Talk radio has been the only place for years you could go to get conservative opinions and presentations, including balanced news. Radio hosts like Rush Limbaugh and Sean Hannity are ultra conservatives, but welcome people with dissenting opinions to call in and say what they want. It is true that they will bring their dissenting view back into what they think it is wrong with it, and leaving the discussion summed up conservatively, but they are respectful to those calling in.

It is certainly incumbent upon us to test what we hear with actual events, and hold these "Fake News" reporters and organizations accountable. Common sense tells us we should not subscribe to biased media, nor watch programs spewing lies and innuendo that they can't back up. At times in

the most extreme cases, we should notify their

advertisers, and stop buying products from those companies who keep advertising on these biased stations. It seems that bias and lies don't matter to advertisers, only money, money, money; sad!

Many so called news websites are quite popular, but it only takes a few minutes of browsing to determine their political affiliation. Once again it is very important that we stay away of the ones that lie and report fake news. Many of them even make up stories to help them fan the flames of discontent, and create a following of people who will accept anything that falls in line with their ideology.

Common sense would tell us not to read, listen to, or watch any news media that reports lies and fabricates stories to support their own agenda's. Advertisers pay attention to numbers, and when circulation falls, viewership drops, and hits on websites trend downward, they will respond in kind. We certainly don't have full control of the medias' financial survivability, but we do have a large effect on who advertises on them, **unless...**

Unless...

Richard L. McBain

CHAPTER TWELVE
Dealing With Crime In America

The horrendous proliferation of crime over the last few decades has been greatly due to ignoring a couple of common sense basic concepts.

1. Repeat criminals are continually let off with a "slap on the hand" or greatly reduced sentences from out of control plea bargaining.

2. Punishment for violent criminals has no teeth in it, and the liberal mentality wants us to coddle these felons instead of making them wish they hadn't done the crimes.

Anyone convicted of a crime should have a price to pay. First-time non-violent convictions should always come with no less than fines, some jail time or enforced community service jobs. Repeat offenders should serve prison time.

First-time violent crimes should get jail time with work attached, and repeat violent criminals should get the maximum sentence for the second or more offenses of the same kind, and prisons should be hell-holes of hard work for violent offenders.

We have prisons in Georgia that are all but run by the gangs incarcerated in them because they have been allowed to become a threatening machine to the guards and their families outside.

Violent gangs outside of prisons should be deemed illegal by legislation that has teeth in it, and belonging to a violent gang should itself be a crime. The terror that these gangs bring to these usually inn-city neighborhoods, has to be stopped by all means necessary. We must allow our police to take down these violent gangs by fighting fire with fire, and with community and government support instead of trying to find ways that the police showed bias and more force than needed.

In prison gangs should not be allowed to form. Common sense should tell us that periodically and regularly gang members should be separated into different prisons, or different buildings within a prison.

Now we come to the second premise of punishment having no teeth in it. What caused the prison systems to ever get away from hard labor? Our prisons need to be involved in making prison life miserable, and a place the prisoners will not want to come back to.

Today the bleeding-heart liberals want prisoners to be in nice, air-conditioned prisons, and not forced to do anything they don't want to do. On the contrary, the prisons allow television, computer time, and even the ability to get a degree on line; what punishment is this for a violent person? This is not working and will never work.

We know the recidivism rate based on the Bureau of Justice Statistics study, for those who are re-arrested within five years after incarceration, is 76.6% from state prisons, and 44.7 re-arrest from federal prisons.

Without bringing back hard labor for violent criminals, we provide these repeat offenders an environment that is better than most of them had, more comfortable, with three meals per day, television, internet time, and many go into gang participation.

Many tell us that the cost of maintaining prisons is astronomical. Common sense says make the prisons pay for themselves. Put prisoners to labor that earns money for the prisons, and don't pay them for working. Instead just give them a nominal weekly allowance to buy their personal needs. Prison ministries are available to help prisoners grow spiritually if they want, and hopefully see the error of their ways.

There will always be crime and repeat offenders, but taking a more, non-liberal punishment with the hard labor approach can greatly aid in many of the ex-cons not wanting to come back, **unless...**

Unless...

CHAPTER THIRTEEN
Common Sense Understanding of Our Constitution and Federal Laws

We have been taught that we need lawyers to interpret the Constitution of the United States, in understanding how it relates to the many legal issues that arise in our country; I say baloney! Of course there are some issues that are not expressly clear and may require legal interpretation, but most of the Constitution is straight forward, and just plain common sense.

For instance, these liberal judges and justices who think they can change existing law because a presidential candidate used what they feel was prejudicial comments during his campaign, have absolutely no right to do so.

Section. 1.

All legislative Powers herein granted shall be vested in a Congress of the United States, which shall consist of a Senate and House of Representatives.

I don't see anything about judges or justices in there; do you?

Tax laws are to be enforced by the IRS, not changed or to show favoritism to one political part or another based on personal ideology. So why hasn't Lois Lerner been charged for breaking the tax laws?

During this last presidential campaign it was discovered that Hillary Clinton blatantly broke the law by putting classified documents on her personal e-mail server. When asked, she expressly denied it. Then those documents were subpoenaed by congress and were willfully withheld. Next Clinton lied under oath repeatedly, but was not prosecuted. Where is the accountability for our leaders who think they are above the law?

As was said earlier, there are Senators like Diane Feinstein, a Democrat liberal from California who made the statement that she thought that our Constitution was a living and evolving document. What a foolish thing to say, and would allow our country's laws to be changed by the whims of whoever holds the most power in Washington.

She made this disingenuous and idiotic comment while being involved in the Senate sub-committee contrived hearings for advice and consent to purposely hold up the confirmation of the Supreme Court candidate Neil Gorsuch. Justice Gorsuch was earlier unanimously approved by her and her cohorts for the 10th Circuit Court of Appeals in 2006.

She again is a prime example of the need for term limits on these entrenched, too old, and I feel corrupt people in Congress. We have them on both sides of the aisle, and America needs to wake up to why this is bad, and stop voting for these relics of the past.

Early immigration law in the Naturalization Act of 1795 contained elements that are still part of our laws. A path to citizenship required that immigrants be of good moral character in line with the Constitution of the United States, and be committed to good order and well being of the U.S., and to take an oath to support the Constitution.

Immigration law today requires competency in the

English language for citizenship, and would disallow those advocate overthrowing our government. Legal immigration is currently set at one million people per year, yet liberals want open boarders. There is no common sense to that except to hopefully get themselves more voters.

It is only common sense that the way to protect our borders from illegal immigrants, drug traffickers, terrorists, and the like is to make it more difficult from them to cross our boarders. A wall may not stop it all, but if constructed properly will certainly make it very difficult. More boarder officers, drone surveillance, and cameras are necessary and greatly helpful. Local and state police need to be empowered to hold the ones they catch for the federal authorities.

As I said earlier, local and state officials who allow sanctuary cities need to ne imprisoned for breaking federal law. Blind as they seem to be, this is called anarchy! Office holders should be held to the same standards as other citizens. When did we ever get to the place where they and wealth people are above the law?

The second amendment gives us the right to bear arms, and I am a complete gun rights advocate. However, even we conservatives need to give in a little to common sense vetting of gun purchasers. Most people have access to immediate background checking at gun stores. If there is a red flag or question, it should not be considered unfair to have to wait a short period to make sure someone isn't getting a gun that shouldn't have one.

So now I step out on a limb and say that the gun show "loophole" should be shored up. Gun show sponsors should provide, maybe for a modest fee, an immediate background check like the gun stores to insure sales are to legitimate people. In this day and age of terrorism, it is just common sense that we step back and rethink security first!

It is obvious that criminals will always find their guns on the black market, but we should make sure that nothing we do can errantly put a gun into the hands of those outside our laws.

Environmentalists have lost their minds ushering certain legislation. The fish VS. farmer debacle in California, that has put some little fishes rights to water more than the farmers whose livelihood depends on that water for their crops; only in California, a no common sense state!

The Obama administration gave over half a billion dollars in loans to Solyndra, a solar panel manufacturer who lied to get the loans, then failed committing fraud on the American people. Wind turbine farms have been mostly a failure, while killing eagles and other endangered species. Environmentalists are fighting natural gas production, fracking, and oil drilling quoting false facts of them endangering our world, while promoting these ridiculous "green" energy operations.

Common sense is non-existent in these far left loons who blame the United States and others on the Global Warming; and no, the science isn't settled at all! The atmosphere changes both up and down, and always has. In the late seventies these same loons were predicting global cooling and the return of the ice age.

All of these common sense problems can be fixed if all of we citizens simply do our part by speaking up and demanding accountability from our leaders. This can change things in a big way **unless...**

Unless...

CHAPTER FOURTEEN
Common Sense Is Easy

It seems like so many people want to make tell us that everything is difficult in life, and so much of the workings are hard to understand; baloney!

Every one of us have common sense if we will be true to it, and not let it get caught up political morass, or what everyone else seems to be doing. God will hold us all accountable when we go before Him, and there won't be any court of appeals, American Law, Feminist Movement, or any other advocate but Jesus!

Whether a person believes it or not, doesn't change the absolute fact that there is only one way to heaven as Jesus said:

Jesus saith unto him, I am the way, the truth, and the life: no man cometh unto the Father, but by me. **John 14:6**

Therefore common sense is easy; it is based on the Word of God found in the Bible. In this holy book we can find the answers to life like what we need to do to be saved, to be decent, and to love our neighbors as ourselves. It tells us we are to combat evil, not to go along to get along.

Common sense is a gift, but many turn from it because they have selfish, self-centered, and self-serving agenda's and don't care about what God said. Here's the common definition:

*Evil, in a general context, is the absence or opposite of that which is described as being good. Often, evil denotes profound immorality.[1] In certain religious contexts, evil has been described as a supernatural force.[1] Definitions of evil vary, as does the analysis of its motives.[2] However, elements that are commonly associated with evil involve unbalanced behavior involving expediency, selfishness, ignorance, or neglect.[3]
* Wikipedia Free Encyclopedia

The very idea of evil being one of the dominating forces in the world has gradually moved from being commonly understood, to one of ridicule, making fun of, and being scoffed at today. If you don't believe in or even recognize evil when you see it, how can you fight it? Evil is the very opposite of good, and most people, no matter what they say, can distinguish good from evil.

The world, and especially the United States has put so much credence on educational degrees and the schools they come from, that they forget what that really means. In modern day thinking a degree, and especially a graduate degree from Ivy League schools impress many people.

For me degrees from Ivy League schools means that they have bought into the secular view of the world in an extremely liberal way. I would prefer, and have hired people with experience and common sense before ever wanting to look at these inflated ego people for the same jobs.

The first man I hired with an MBA from a so called good school took me six months to break him out of that unrealistic ideology he had been taught. He finally came to me one day without the steepling of his fingers, he said, "I have been a real ass____ haven't I?" I told him that yes he had. He asked me why did I keep him then, and I told him that I saw real potential in him if he would just drop the college arrogance. He did, and he became a very productive employee.

It is time for all of us to rely more on common sense than ideology taught by people with an ax to grind. Common sense can be developed through the regular study of God's Word. Remember, even the non-believers don't call it the good book for nothing!

Richard L. McBain

About the Author

Richard L. McBain

Dick McBain, 75, speaks about what an incredible life God has blessed him with. He and Jackie have been married for 52 years, and raised two boys Dan and Mike who have provided them two grandchildren each.

Dick has been a corporate executive for over thirty-five years, and is the CEO of Triune Group, Inc. a consulting and publishing company. He is the author of twenty-six published books, a public speaker, and the Atlanta Chapter President of Full Gospel Business Men's Fellowship in America™.

Dick has watched the great demise of the United States over the last decade or so, and laments that his grandchildren will never know the fun and happiness of growing up like he did in the nineteen fifties and sixties. Then kids played outside most of their lives, and participated in sport games, swimming, skating, and interacting with their friends.

He has watched as young adults became wanton and gave up the responsibility of raising their children, so both parents could work and earn more money. They stopped taking them to church for spiritual training largely due to not wanting to hear themselves what God has to say about families.

Kids were then reared by daycare centers lacking the love they desperately needed in their young, formative years. The found out how to fend for themselves, and today use the social media to communicate with friends. As a result, kids today have no idea how to socialize, negotiate, and have fun playing outside.

Besides the kids, Dick has seen the demise of being neighborly. Society has bred narcissism and self-centeredness, not caring about others, and buying into the lie that all of this is okay.

The Liberal-Progressive Movement is destroying our schools by promoting socialistic ideas, and being intolerant of any dissenting views. Common Sense has been replaced by pure ideological hogwash, and the problems as a result are going on and on.

Dick decided to write this book as a help to seeing a new direction. He believes we can turn things around in a big way, and gives some ideas as to what we need to do. He believes everyone should feel a responsibility to deal with what they can control, and feels that will turn things significantly around, **unless...**

Richard L. McBain

Other Books
By Richard L. -McBain

< Itching Ears – the great apostacy

Deliverer In Our> Midst – all about the Holy Spirit

< Reluctant Warrior true Vietnam Combat experiences
Are You Going To > Heaven

< The Babyboomer Revolution true stories from author
Are You Being Led> to the Spiritual Slaughter

 < Angels Unawares
Stories of Angels

Darkness Beaten Novel>
A teenage Champion fights
demons

 <Dude, Lying Isn't
Cool
Cheating Hurts Yourself >
And Others

 <Proper Manners
Will Help People
Like You
Respect And >
Obedience Stand
Out

 <Imagining How It
Must Have Been- True
History with a fictitious
character
Jungle Fighters >
Jungle Combat

<By The Word Of Our
Testimony And The
Blood Of The Lamb
Joy Makes Us > Strong

<Do You Know What
God Said?
Prophecy proves>
That The Bible Is The
Word Of God

<Ancestry Tales Of
Three Families
True Stories
The Adventures> Of
Beau

<Teen Detective
Team Mystery
Series
Why Only God>
Can Save The
American Way

<Unless – a case for
common sense

The Neighborhood>
Kids

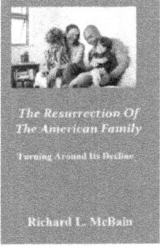

<The Resurrection
Of The American
Family
Christianity >
Questions And
Answers

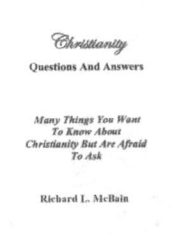

<A Guide For
Ministering
Deliverance

Unless...